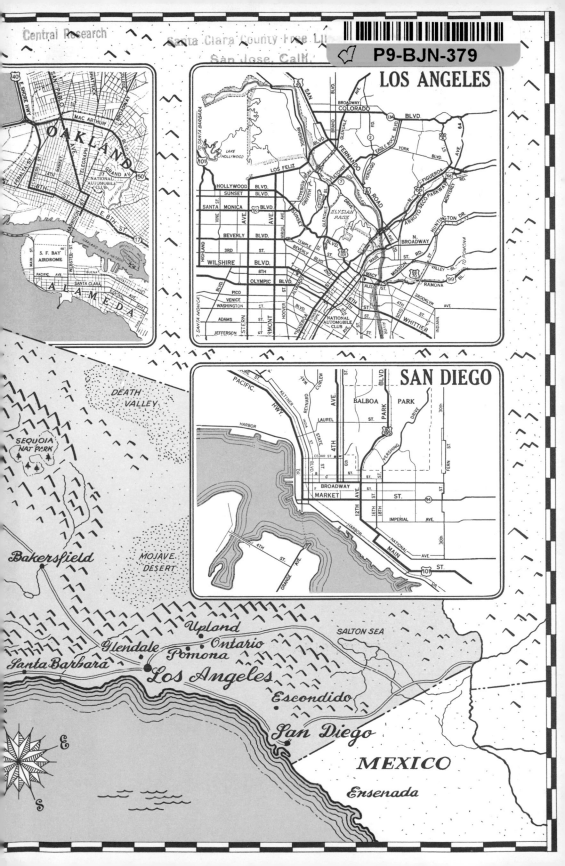

Cordially
Merrill A Reed

HISTORICAL

STATUES & MONUMENTS
in

CALIFORNIA

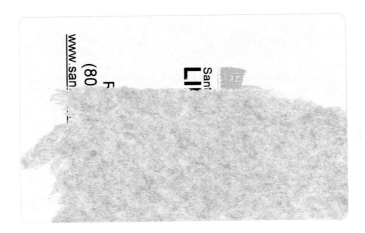

BY MERRILL A. REED

LITHOGRAPHED IN THE U.S.A., JUNE, 1956 BY

MERRILL REED

414 JACKSON STREET, SAN FRANCISCO 11, CALIFORNIA

This book is gratefully dedicated to
those who gave so freely of their time
and effort to make this project a reality

Introduction and Credits

The reader looking for a literary achievement in this book is doomed to disappointment, but he will not have to read far before he realizes the vast amount of work and research necessary to tell even so briefly the fascinating story of the men and women whom the statues commemorate, and to credit properly the deserving sculptors and donors who made the statues possible. Standard encyclopaedias, biographies and histories have been consulted, and occasionally quoted, but such works do not give names of the man or men who inspired the creation of the statues, nor the names of the artists who sculptored them, nor the essentials of WHO, WHY, WHEN and WHERE. It is the purpose of this book to do just that!

Such a vast enterprise could not have been completed without the help of a multitude of heads and hands, and to those who enthusiastically gave their time and effort the editor extends his sincerest thanks: To Miriam Feild for her wholehearted investigation and research; to Louise Lawrence of the California State Automobile Association, whose "all points" bulletins brought invaluable information; William Elsner of the California Palace of the Legion of Honor; Veda Y. Conning of the San Francisco Park and Recreation Department; Jack Shwarder, California State Division of Parks and Playgrounds; F. W. Roewekamp, Superintendent of Park Development, Los Angeles; Gardner Morse, Convention and Tourist Bureau, San Diego; Clyde Arbuckle, Secretary, Historic Landmarks Commission, San Jose; Mrs. W. M. O'Donnell, Secretary, History and Art Association, Monterey; Anna Dietz, Hartnell College, Salinas. And especial thanks to Robert Hays of the Escondido Chamber of Commerce, who provided Ted Krec's photograph of the monument and his own thrilling story of the battle of San Pasqual; Harry Rowe of the Solano County Free Library, Fairfield, who provided the inspiring material from which the brief sketch of Chief Solano was taken. Guy Crowe of Madera deserves deep appreciation for his visit to our office to relate the history of the Savage monument and the legend of the Mystery Angel; John Mulkey, Union-Tribune, San Diego; Keith Emenegger, News-Tribune, Madera; Walter Kane, Bakersfield Californian, Bakersfield; C. B. Otis, Eureka Newspapers, Inc., Eureka; L. R. Petithomme, editor, Prospect-Tribune, Calaveras, and to James M. Cardwell of Forest Lawn Memorial Park, Glendale. And heartfelt thanks to Elizabeth Thomas, Oakland; Joyce Zechar, Los Angeles; Barbara Davis, Sacramento, and Dick Moore, Fresno—all with the Chambers of Commerce of their respective cities. And to Frank Thomas, photographer, sincere thanks for service far beyond the call of duty. And many thanks to Phelps Dewey, San Francisco Chronicle promotion director, for the architect's drawing of Bufano's statue, "PEACE." This statue is a gift to San Francisco from the Chronicle, to be erected at the city's International Airport.

Authorities consulted for the backgrounds of individuals whose commemorative statues and monuments are pictured herein, and from which we have abstracted and occasionally quoted, are the following: Encyclopaedia Britannica; "California's Stately Hall of Fame," Hunt; San Francisco's "Chronicle" and "Examiner"; "Comstock Commotion," Beebe; "They Were San Franciscans," Miriam Allen deFord; "From Wilderness to Empire," Wilder; "Streets of San Francisco," Dickson.

If any of our history-minded readers are interested in further reading concerning the men and women and the subjects so briefly covered herein, a list of recommended authorities is included in the appendix.

TABLE OF CONTENTS

TABLE OF CONTENTS (cont.)

TABLE OF CONTENTS (cont.)

TABLE OF CONTENTS (cont.)

American Indian

This is no particular Indian, but a majestic statue by the late Arthur Putnam of the type of the North American Indian found by the pioneers in San Diego. It stands in San Diego's Presidio Park and was a gift from the Scripps Estate to the City.

At the time Cabrillo landed in San Diego some of the Indians were very friendly and cooperative; on the other hand, at different times and places, they were hostile and dangerous.

Father Junipero Serra, founder of twenty-one missions in California, and Father Francisco Garces, the intrepid explorer, earned the Indians' respect and confidence, but Father Garces was eventually slain, together with some members of the Spanish settlements because the whites could no longer provide them with supplies and presents.

Photo: Courtesy California Palace of the Legion of Honor.

Combat-Man, Puma and Cub

1 This bronze sculpture by the late Arthur Putnam is in the California Palace of the Legion of Honor. It was a gift from Mrs. A. B. Spreckels.

American Indian 2

Chief Solano

This statue of Chief Solano, an Indian who had a county named for him, stands on Highway 40 in Fairfield, California. Mary Jean Davis, in a masterful story in the California Highway Patrolman's Magazine has the following to say:

"A 12 foot bronze statue by William Gordon Huff was erected in commemoration of the great life of Chief Solano through the efforts of the Order of Native Sons, Red Men and Pocahontas of California. To Senators Herbert W. Slater of Santa Rosa and Thomas McCormick of Rio Vista goes the credit for getting a bill passed in the legislature assisting in the raising of funds for this monument.

"Chief Solano was given a commission in the Spanish army. He was an aide to General Vallejo and a great help to the American government in keeping the peace between the Indians and white settlers. The American government granted him extensive landholdings, out of which he was ultimately mulcted by white settlers.

"It was a sad mistake, and it is to the white man's credit that he regrets it. It is also to his credit that after one hundred and seventeen years, he is unwilling that the white men forget the debt he owes to this great Indian.

"After one hundred and seventeen years the white man erects to the Red Man a monument in memory of qualities that are never old . . ."

3

PHOTO: CONWAY STUDIO, FAIRFIELD

Chief Solano

4

Juan Rodriguez Cabrillo

This monument to Cabrillo was sent as a gift to the United States from Portugal, and now stands in Balboa Park, San Diego.

In the first Spanish venture to find what was "beyond the Lower California Peninsula", Juan Rodriguez Cabrillo, a Portuguese adventurer who had played the role of conquistador under Narvaez, Orozco and Alvarado, was placed in command of the expedition because he had "served his Majesty well in every way that offered, and was well versed in navigation."

Cabrillo's command consisted of two ships, the San Salvador and the Victoria. "The vessels," wrote George Davidson, "were smaller than any of our coasting schooners." Second in command was Bartolome Ferrelo, a native of the Levant who, like his commander, proved to be a man of courage and determination, and very "skilled in all the affairs of the sea."

On September 27, 1542, the Spaniards sailed past the inhospitable Coronado Islands, and the following morning, a Thursday, they entered San Diego harbor—"a port closed and very good, which they called San Miguel." Here a detachment went ashore "where there were some people. Three of them waited, but all of the rest of them fled. To these three they gave some presents and they said by signs that in the interior people like the Spaniards had passed. They gave signs of great fear."

Thus, in language as terse and simple as that of an Old Testament narrative, the chronicler describes the historic discovery of California and San Diego.

5

Cabrillo, Balboa Park

6

Cabrillo, Point Loma

This monument commemorating Juan Rodriguez Cabrillo is located on Point Loma, San Diego, and is a part of State Monument No. 51, the old Spanish lighthouse which originally was located on Point Loma having been replaced by a modern lighthouse near this monument to Cabrillo.

Rockwell D. Hunt tells us in his book, "California's Stately Hall of Fame," that "California's recorded history begins in 1542, a scant fifty years after Columbus discovered America. It was on the twenty-eighth day of September of that year that Juan Rodriguez Cabrillo, a skilled mariner of Portuguese birth, sailing under Spanish colors, brought his two tiny ships into San Diego, 'a port closed and very good', which he named San Miguel."

Each year on September 28, the anniversary of the landing in San Diego Bay is celebrated as "Cabrillo Day" and is generally observed by the people of California. Cabrillo remained in San Diego about six days, then proceeded northward.

Photo: Courtesy California Palace of the Legion of Honor.

Puma Devouring a Rabbit

7

This bronze piece is a gift from Mrs. A. B. Spreckels to the California Palace of the Legion of Honor. Sculptored by the late Arthur Putnam.

HERE · AT POINT LOMA
HEAD · ON THE AFTERNOON
OF SEPTEMBER 28 1542
JUAN RODRIGUEZ
CABRILLO
DISTINGUISHED PORTUGUESE
NAVIGATOR
IN
THE SERVICE OF SPAIN
COMMANDING THE FLAG
SHIP SAN SALVADOR MADE
HIS FIRST ALTA CALI
FORNIA LANDFALL AND
THUS DISCOVERED WHAT
IS NOW THE STATE OF
CALIFORNIA
CABRILLO · WITH HIS COM
PANIONS · CAME ASHORE
ON POINT LOMA AT WHAT
IS NOW BALLAST POINT
IN THIS PORT 'CLOSED
AND VERY GOOD' WHICH
THEY NAMED SAN MIGUEL

CABRILLO'S CARAVELS ·
ASSEMBLED AT NAVIDAD
MEXICO UNDER ORDERS OF
DON ANTONIO DE MENDOZA ·
SAILED FROM THAT PORT
JUNE 27 1542

Cabrillo, Point Loma

8

Prayer Book Cross

The Prayer Book Cross was a gift to San Francisco's Golden Gate Park in 1894 by George W. Childs of Philadelphia. The first religious service held in California in the English language was celebrated by Francis Fletcher, Chaplain of Drake's ship, the Golden Hind, on the shore of Drake's Bay, June 24, 1579; the Prayer Book Cross was erected in commemoration of that event. The voyage around the world, during which Sir Francis Drake cruised along the Pacific Coast as far as 49 North, was the first ever made by an Englishman.

Cross, Trinidad Head

Captain Bruno Hecata, with the ship Santiago, and Lieutenant Juan Francisco de Bodega y Cuadra brought their vessels into Trinidad Bay on June 9, 1775. Two days later a landing was made, the Spanish banner unfurled, and Father Miguel de la Campa celebrated Mass. The day was Trinity Sunday, which accounts for the name given the Bay. The clubwomen of Humboldt County marked the site of the Spanish landing with this permanent Cross.

Historic Cross, Olvera Street

This historical Cross commemorates the founding of Los Angeles, and is inscribed, "El Pueblo de Nuestra Senora la Reina de Los Angeles, September 4, 1781, Felipe de Neve."

Prayer Book Cross   10

CAROLUS III. Dei G. Hyspaniarum Rex

JUNE 9, 1775

REPLACED BY
CLUB WOMEN OF
HUMBOLDT CO.
SEPT. 9, 1913

PHOTO: HUMBOLDT STANDARD, EUREKA

11   **Trinidad Head**

Cross, Olvera Street, Los Angeles   12

JUNIPERO SERRA, San Diego,
1713 - 1784

This statue of Junipero Serra is in San Diego's Presidio Park, and is the work of the late Arthur Putnam, one of California's most celebrated sculptors. It was a gift to the City of San Diego by the E. W. Scripps Estate. On July 16, 1769, Father Serra founded the Mission San Diego de Alcala, it being the first of 21 Franciscan Missions subsequently founded in the State.

JUNIPERO SERRA, Monterey

This statue of Father Serra is on the spot where he landed June 3, 1770, and founded the Mission San Carlos, Monterey. The statue is a gift of Jane L. Stanford, and was erected in the Presidio of Monterey in 1891.

JUNIPERO SERRA, San Francisco

This impressive statue of Father Serra is in San Francisco's Golden Gate Park at the junction of Academy of Science and Court Drives. The bronze figure of Father Serra is the work of Douglas Tilden, and the base upon which it stands is the design of architect Edgar Mathews. Father Serra founded the Mission Dolores in San Francisco, October 9, 1776.

JUNIPERO SERRA, Mission Dolores

This figure of Father Serra is located in San Francisco's Mission Dolores. It is a part of a group originally planned for the E. W. Scripps Estate by San Francisco's noted sculptor, the late Arthur Putnam. Father Serra was born in Majorca, in 1713, and died at San Carlos Mission, Carmel Valley, California, August 27, 1784, and is buried there.

13

PHOTO: BISHOP NEWSPHOTOS, SAN DIEGO

Junipero Serra, San Diego   14

15   **Junipero Serra**, Monterey

PADRE
JVNIPERO
SERRA
FOVNDER
OF·THE·
CALIFORNIA
·MISSIONS·
1713-1784

Junipero Serra, San Francisco   16

17   **Junipero Serra,** Mission Dolores

MADONNA OF THE TRAIL

N·S·D·A·R· MEMORIAL
TO THE
PIONEER MOTHERS
OF THE
COVERED WAGON·DAYS

PIONEER MOTHERS

This imposing statue is in Upland, and portrays the Pioneer Mother with bonnet and babe in arms. It was the pioneer Mothers who did much in building up California's frontiers.

18

Felipe de Neve
1740 - 1784

Parlor No. 247 of the Native Daughters of the Golden West gave this statue of California's first "law giver" to the City of Los Angeles, which he founded in 1781. The statue is the work of Henry Lion, and is in the center of the Plaza on North Main Street, where it is viewed daily by the thousands of Latin Americans who visit the "Church of Our Lady of the Angels", the oldest building in Los Angeles, which stands directly opposite.

Rockwell Hunt, author of "California's Stately Hall of Fame," has the following to say of de Neve: "Of the ten Spanish governors of California, beginning with Portola, the greatest in administrative ability, personal energy and statesmanlike foresight was Felipe de Neve. As a young man, de Neve arrived in New Spain (Mexico) a few years before the beginning of actual occupation of Alta California by Captain Gaspar de Portolá and Padre Junipero Serra...

"Had Felipe de Neve accomplished nothing else ... he should be gratefully remembered for having drawn up the memorable Reglamento with which his name will always be associated. It comprises 'Regulations for the Government of the Province of California by Don Felipe de Neve, Governor of the same, dated in the Royal Presidio of San Carlos de Monterey, 1st June, 1779, and approved by his Majesty in a royal order of the 24th October, 1781'."

PHOTO: COURTESY CHAMBER OF COMMERCE, LOS ANGELES

Felipe de Neve

20

Juan Bautista de Anza
Born 1735

"As an explorer" writes Bancroft, "de Anza easily deserves to rank among many who have been awarded more conspicuous places in history". Juan Bautista de Anza had spent a great part of his life in dreaming of opening a route to Alta California. In 1772 he petitioned the Viceroy to permit him to organize and lead an expedition to California, and offered to meet most of the expense himself. In 1773, Bucareli approved de Anza's overland route from Sonora and commissioned de Anza to organize and command the party. In addition to the usual pack train of provisions and supplies, the party took along a large herd of horses and cattle. From Caborca, the last civilized settlement on the frontier, he followed the fairly well traveled but extremely dangerous route commonly called El Camino del Diablo, to the Colorado-Gila junction. There he was lucky to cement the friendship with Salvador Palma, chief of the Yuma Indians, that Garcés had started several years before. Having decorated Palma and gained his cooperation and friendship, the route between Sonora and California remained open until trouble broke out between the Spaniards and the Yuma Indians. Subsequently descending into a valley above the present city of San Jacinto, he continued on a trail that ran through Riverside, the Santa Ana river, the Arroyo of the Bears, Ontario and the San Gabriel River. Finally, on March 22, two months after leaving Caborca, he knocked on the gates of the San Gabriel Mission.

21

TO THE HONOR AND GLORY
OF
JUAN BAUTISTA D'ANZA
TRAILMAKER
AND HIS BAND OF INTREPID FOLLOWERS
WHO ON
MARCH 21, 1774
PASSED NEAR THIS SPOT ON THEIR WAY
TO
SAN GABRIEL AND MONTEREY
THE FIRST WHITE MEN TO BREAK A TRAIL
OVERLAND TO CALIFORNIA

THIS MEMORIAL PLACED BY
THE BOY SCOUT AND SERVICE ORGANIZATIONS
OF ONTARIO
FEBRUARY 8, 1930

FRASHERS PHOTO, POMONA

Juan Bautista de Anza   22

Padre Francisco Garcés

This statue of the Franciscan missionary, the first known white man in the area, is the work of the sculptor John Palo'Kangas, and stands in the city of Bakersfield where it was erected by the efforts of citizens, service clubs and the Chamber of Commerce. It was dedicated March 7, 1939.

Few historians have given proper recognition to Padre Francisco Garcés "for what he was or what he did." Garcés was a trail blazer of determination and courage, friendly with the hostile Indians and a Christian martyr. Separating from de Anza's column, Garcés set out to explore a route from the Colorado to Monterey. Garcés had a rare ability to make friends of primitive people. With two companions the intrepid Garcés plunged into the lonely wastes of the Colorado desert which no white man had ever seen before. Garcés reached San Gabriel March 24, threaded his way through the Sierra Madre and Tehachapi Mountains, and eventually came out in the San Joaquin Valley. Turning back at the northern boundary of Kern County, he found his way across hundreds of miles of trackless desert, traveling in all, 2400 miles in 11 months.

Garcés was massacred in 1781 by the Yuma Indians, because the padres were no longer able to give them supplies and presents.

Father Garcés

24

George Washington

This statue of George Washington is in San Francisco's Veterans Memorial Building, and is a replica of the one done in 1786 by Jean Antoine Houdon, the celebrated French sculptor. His commission to execute the statue of Washington was from the Legislature of Virginia. Putting aside other important commissions, Houdon journeyed to the United States with Benjamin Franklin in 1785 and spent considerable time with George Washington at Mount Vernon modeling the bust. He completed the statue in France. Jean Antoine Houdon was born in Versailles, March, 1740. At 12 he entered the Ecole Royale de Sculpture, and at 20, having learned all that he could from Michel Ange Slodtz and Pigalle, he carried off the Prix de Rome and left France for Italy, where he spent the next ten years of his life. Eight years later he was admitted to the French Academy. To every salon Houdon was a chief contributor; most of the leading men of the day were his sitters. The Revolution broke up the busy flow of commissions, and Houdon then took up a half-forgotten project for a statue of St. Scholastica. He was immediately denounced to the convention, and his life was saved by his instant and ingenious adaptation of St. Scholastica into an embodiment of Philosophy. He did busts of Marshall Ney, Catherine, and of Napoleon himself, by whom Houdon was rewarded with the Legion of Honor. He died in Paris, July 16, 1828.

George Washington

26

Benjamin Franklin
1706 - 1790

This statue of Benjamin Franklin, in San Francisco's Washington Square, is best known as the "Cogswell Historical Moument", because an inscription on it says "Presented by H. D. Cogswell to our Boys and Girls who will soon take our places as we pass on" and also refers to the "Historical Society in 1879".

Ben Franklin, the "patron saint" of the country's printing industry, was born in erudite Boston, July 6, 1706, at a time when Boston was a "thriving, growing and promising city of 5,000 souls."

Many firsts are credited to Franklin; among other things, he founded the first circulating library in the country, but his most successful venture was probably "Poor Richard's Almanac" as is proved by the innumerable translations and reprints. In 1900 there were 75 English editions, 56 French, 11 German and 9 Italian.

His unabated zeal for the welfare of mankind led him to publish in the last months of his life several papers on behalf of the abolition of slavery.

> "* * * WHEN MEN DIFFER IN OPINION, BOTH SIDES OUGHT EQUALLY TO HAVE THE ADVANTAGE OF BEING HEARD IN PUBLIC; AND THAT WHEN TRUTH AND ERROR HAVE FAIR PLAY, THE FORMER IS ALWAYS AN OVERMATCH FOR THE OTHER"
>
> BENJAMIN FRANKLIN

Benjamin Franklin   28

PHOTO: FRANK J. THOMAS

GENERAL LAFAYETTE

This life size statue of the French hero who helped out America during Revolutionary War days, is by sculptor Arnold Foerster, and stands in Lafayette Park in Los Angeles. It was dedicated March 30, 1937.

29

PHOTO: FRANK J. THOMAS

LEIF ERIKSON

This statue of the Scandinavian explorer, whose saga says was the son of "Eric the Red," was executed by Nina Saemundssenn, and it stands at the Western Avenue entrance to Griffith Park in Los Angeles.

30

Bear Flag Monument

The dedication plaque on the statue says: "This monument was erected by the Native Sons of the Golden West and the State of California to commemorate the raising of the 'Bear Flag' on this spot June 1846 by the Bear Flag party and their declaration of the freedom of California from Mexico. On July 9, 1846, the Bear Flag was hauled down and the American Flag raised in its place by Lieutenant Joseph W. Revere, U.S.A. who was sent to Sonoma from San Francisco by Commander John B. Montgomery of the United States sloop of war, "Portsmouth", following the raising of the Flag at Monterey, July 7, 1846, by Commodore John Drake Sloat.

It is said that the original Bear Flag, one of the State's most interesting relics, was destroyed in the San Francisco earthquake and fire, but the memory of that flag and the traditions that clustered around it will not grow dim in the minds of Californians.

Photo: Courtesy California Palace of the Legion of Honor.

Lioness and Snakes

31 Mrs. A. B. Spreckels presented this bronze sculpture by the late Arthur Putnam to the California Palace of the Legion of Honor.

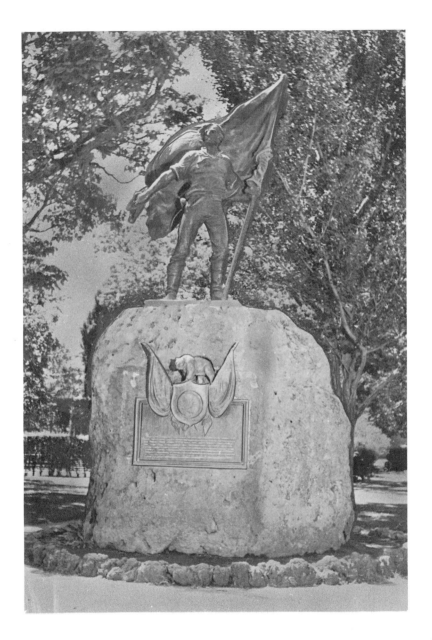

Bear Flag Monument   32

Francis Scott Key

This huge statue of Francis Scott Key, author of "The Star Spangled Banner", stands in San Francisco's Golden Gate Park, in front of the Steinhart Aquarium courtyard. It is the work of William Westmore Story, and was given to the city in 1887 by James Lick.

Francis Scott Key was born in Frederick County, Maryland, and graduated from St. John's College. In 1801 he began the practice of law in the city of his birth.

Subsequently moving to Washington, D. C., he was that city's district attorney for three terms. In 1814 Key visited the British fleet in Chesapeake Bay in an attempt to secure the release of a friend who had been captured. He was detained during the shelling of Fort McHenry, one of the forts defending Baltimore. During the night's shelling, Key's anxiety was at high pitch and, when in the morning he saw the American Flag still flying over the fort, he gave vent to his feelings in "The Star Spangled Banner". The song became immediately popular, and on March 3, 1931, it was made our national anthem by Act of Congress.

THEN CONQUER WE MUST—FOR OUR CAUSE IT IS JUST,—
AND THIS BE OUR MOTTO,—"IN GOD IS OUR TRUST!"

FRANCIS SCOTT KEY

Francis Scott Key   34

Memorial Tablet to Bret Harte

On the opposite page is reproduced the tablet on the south wall of the Bohemian Club in memory of Bret Harte. It is the work of Joseph J. Mora. You know the figures that make his books alive—here they are stepping forth into living bronze—gambler and dance hall girl, rough miner and tender pioneer woman—pictures of early days worth more to the State than the gold they came to seek.

To the memory of Bret Harte, who wrote of San Francisco as "Serene, indifferent of Fate", a memorial tablet was unveiled with appropriate ceremonial by the Bohemian Club, August 15, 1919.

"The tablet is the work of Joseph J. Mora, the sculptor. It portrays, in bas relief, many of the figures whom Bret Harte has made immortal in his writings, ranging from 'Kentuck', the great-hearted miner who gave his life to save the baby known the the 'Luck' of Roaring Camp, to Mother Shipton and the Duchess, outcasts of Poker Flat, and from 'Tennessee's Pardner', uncouth but faithful, to 'Miggles', the Magdalene of Bret Harte's stories, and to that 'Heathen Chinee', whose 'ways are dark, and whose tricks are vain'." *From the San Francisco Examiner, August 16, 1919.*

"ONE GREAT VICE IN A MAN IS APT TO KEEP OUT A GREAT MANY SMALL ONES."

BRET HARTE

35

Bret Harte Plaque

36

Robert Burns
1759 - 1796

This statue of the celebrated Scottish poet is on the Main Drive of San Francisco's Golden Gate Park. It is the work of sculptor Earl Cummings and the statue was donated to the city by the Scots of San Francisco. Burns' first volume was published in June, 1786, at Kilmarnock, Scotland.

Robert Emmet
1778 - 1803

This statue of Robert Emmet, the celebrated Irish patriot, is in San Francisco's Golden Gate Park, on the Academy of Science Drive, south of the Aquarium. Emmet entered Trinity College, Dublin, in October, 1793. He resigned from the college as a protest against the inquisitorial examination of the political views of the students. James D. Phelan presented the statue to the city and at the dedication ceremonies the speaker was de Valera, President of the Irish Republic.

Commodore John Drake Sloat
1781 - 1867

The picture on page 40 is of the Sloat Monument in the Presidio of Monterey. The monument is the result of 20 years of effort on the part of Major E. A. Sherman, one of the three remaining veterans of the Mexican War. The U. S. Senate appropriated $10,000 for the completion of this monument. Sloat arrived in Monterey aboard his flagship, the "Savannah," July 2, 1846, and five days later, after consultation with Larkin, landed a detachment of Marines, raised the American Flag and declared California a possession of the United States.

Robert Burns   38

39   Robert Emmet

Commodore Sloat   40

St. Francis of Assisi

On the steps of San Francisco second oldest church, at the intersection of Montgomery Avenue and Vallejo Street, is this modernistic 12-ton statue of St. Francis, with the following inscription:

ST. FRANCIS OF ASSISI
Patron of the City
Monumental Shrine
Beniamino Bufano, Sculptor
Benefaction of Annunziata Sanguinetti
MCMLV

Bufano's 18-foot Swedish granite statue was dedicated October 4, 1955, with the Most Reverend Merlin Guilfoyle blessing the statue before a large crowd. Following the blessing, a Solemn High Mass was celebrated by the Reverend Alvin Wagner, pastor of the church.

Bufano finished this statue 27 years ago, and it was left to gather dust in a warehouse in Paris while a dozen civic controversies raged. With the financial and moral help of art lovers and loyal church members, the statue was redeemed from storage and arrived in San Francisco in June, 1955.

One leading art critic said it is "the most significant piece of sculpture done within the past 500 years."

41

St. Francis, Bufano   42

St. Francis, Huntington

This life size bronze statue of St. Francis was executed by sculptor Clara Huntington of San Francisco. It was Miss Huntington who did the marble bas-relief of H. E. Huntington, now in Huntington Library, San Marino, California. In a letter to the San Francisco Chronicle, Mrs. Charles H. Bull of San Mateo stated:

"To me, and I feel sure to many others, it was one of the most inspiring and beautiful works of art at the fair. With Shasta daisies or other flowers surrounding it and water pouring from upturned, outstretched hands, the bronze statue seemed to signify all that was good and compassionate and radiated a feeling of peace found in too few places today.

"Golden Gate Park seems a fitting place where in quiet, peaceful surroundings it would continue to inspire passersby and be appreciated by all. We hope that others will join in an effort to have this work of art brought out of the dark and into the light."

Mme. Helena Modjeska

Polish by birth—an American citizen by choice—Helena Modjeska, acclaimed as "the world's greatest tragedienne," made her debut in San Francisco, and in between theatrical tours she made her home in Anaheim and Orange county, California. Santiago Canyon in the Santa Ana mountains became Modjeska's "Forest of Arden." After her retirement she found a new home on the small island of East Newport, on the shores of the Pacific. It was here that she died on April 8, 1909. The citizens of Anaheim have memorialized her in an imposing statue standing at the northwest entrance to its city park.

43

St. Francis, Huntington   44

PHOTO: ANAHEIM BULLETIN

Memorial to Mme. Modjeska
Anaheim

45

GOLD MINER'S MONUMENT This statue is by Henry Lion. It is in the Carthay Center Parkway in Los Angeles. It was donated by J. Harvey McCarthy and was dedicated in 1927 under the auspices of the Grand Parlor of Native Sons of the Golden West.

46

Savage Monument

This monument, erected on the grave of Major James D. Savage, is on the River Road, about 15 miles northeast of Madera, California. It was brought around the Horn from Connecticut by a sailing vessel and transported to the site by ox cart. Major Savage was the discoverer of Yosemite Valley, and was chiefly engaged in quelling Indian uprisings and relocating the Indians on government reservations.

Mystery Angel

No one living knows definitely why, by whom, or when this rapidly deteriorating figure was done, or how. Legendary tales claim that it was carved by a talented sculptor who, in the 30's or 40's, was in a party of trappers who came over from Salt Lake Valley and camped on this site. Ultimately captured and imprisoned by the authorities at Monterey, and subsequently released, they retraced their journey and, camping on the same place, carved their initials and the date. What is left of the statue is on the property of Herrick Brown, whose ownership of the property is through inheritance from his father and grandfather.

Totem Pole
"Guardian of the Forest"

This noteworthy Totem Pole, "modern style," was carved out of a solid tree by Dudley C. Carter at the Golden Gate International Exposition on Treasure Island, San Francisco. An axe was his only tool. It is in San Francisco's Golden Gate Park on the Main Drive, at Lindley Meadows.

47

TO THE MEMORY
OF MAJ.
JAMES D. SAVAGE

Savage Monument   48

49   **Mystery Angel**

Guardian of the Forest   50

Mark Twain

1835 - 1910

This statue of Mark Twain is located in Angels Camp in the Mother Lode country, and the names of its sculptor and donor are completely forgotten by historians and old timers alike.

Samuel Langhorne Clemens, better known by his pen name, "Mark Twain" was born in Florida, Missouri, November 30, 1835. After learning the printer's trade and something of steamboating, he drifted west with his brother, Orion, who had just been appointed Lieutenant Governor of Nevada.

The publication of the "Jumping Frog of Calaveras County" made Mark Twain famous overnight. Nevada claims him, too. In his recent book, "Comstock Commotion", Lucius Beebe, present owner of the Territorial Enterprise, states that "ninety years later, the inheritors of the Territorial Enterprise's fortunes were fond of referring to the property upon occasion as the literary birthplace of Mark Twain."

Mark Twain was most popular in his own day as a humorist, but he will survive rather as the master folkwriter of the pioneering epoch who has left in "Roughing It" and "Life on the Mississippi" unrivaled pictures of the character and manners of the Middle and Far West in Civil War days.

> "A CLASSIC IS SOMETHING EVERYBODY WANTS TO BE READ AND NOBODY WANTS TO READ."
>
> MARK TWAIN

PHOTO: HILLCREST STUDIO, ANGELS CAMP

Mark Twain

52

Donner Pioneer Monument
Donner Lake

This historic monument is located at Donner Lake, about three miles west of Truckee on U. S. Highway 40. This is State Monument No. 134, and commemorates the heroism and the tragedy of a westbound party of emigrants who were trapped in the snow from October 1846 to April 1847.

The story of the Donner party is one of the most gripping tales in the annals of California. The fortitude and devotion of the brave men and women are unbelievable. The party started from Sangamon County, Illinois, and consisted, among others, of three families: George Donner, his wife, and five children; Jacob Donner, his wife, and seven children; James Reed, his wife, and four children; and ninety-year-old Sarah Keyes, the mother of Mrs. Reed.

In October they reached what was to be later called Donner Lake in the high Sierra. They became snow bound and sent out a party for aid. This party never returned. The second relief expedition, consisting of Brit Greenwood, William McCutchen and James Reed, set out for aid, taking two Reed children and another boy. They succeeded in bringing back food to the dying emigrants.

This was probably the worst catastrophe in the history of westward emigration.

Donner Monument

54

James Wilson Marshall
1810 - 1885

Marshall, whom history credits with California's first gold discovery, was born in Hunderstown, N. Y., and subsequently found his way to California via an emigrant party from Oregon about the year 1844. He was a wheelwright by trade and entered the employ of John A. Sutter, whose settlement at New Helvetia was growing.

Convinced that there would be a demand for good flour, Sutter began in 1847 the construction of a flour mill about five miles from his fort. He delegated Marshall to build a sawmill on the south fork of the American River, with which it was planned to manufacture lumber for the flour mill.

The sawmill was erected where now stands the town of Coloma. It was necessary to deepen the tail race at the sawmill, and after the change was made gold was found in the waters running from the tail race.

Marshall told Sutter of the discovery, and the two of them endeavored to claim larger landholdings, but were thwarted by Governor Mason at Monterey, who told them he was powerless until the Congress passed a law, or the President issued a proclamation respecting land titles. This started a losing fight that the two men waged for years to hold possession of certain lands. Both men lost everything and died in want.

PHOTO: COURTESY EL DORADO COUNTY CHAMBER OF COMMERCE, PLACERVILLE

Marshall Monument   56

GENERAL HARRISON GRAY OTIS

This monument by Prince Paul Troubetzky is in MacArthur Park, Los Angeles. Soldier, journalist and top-flight citizen, he was co-founder and publisher of the Los Angeles Times, a factor in building Southern California.

57

PIONEER MOTHER   The Native Daughters of the Golden West placed this statue by Charles Grafly in San Francisco's Golden Gate Park in 1940. It is on the Main Drive at the entrance to Stow Lake.

MADONNA AND CHILD

59

This statue is the property of the Los Angeles County Museum of Art. It is by a 15th century anonymous Burgundian sculptor, given to the museum by Duveen Brothers of New York.

ST. ELIZABETH OF HUNGARY

This Lindenwood carving is by an unknown sculptor of the Franco-Thuringian school. It is the property of the California Palace of the Legion or Honor.

60

Thomas Starr King, French
1824-1864

This statue of the Unitarian clergyman is the work of Daniel Chester French and is on the Main Drive of San Francisco's Golden Gate Park.

This statue of the Boston and San Francisco clergyman who is credited with playing a large part in saving California for the Union at the outbreak of the Civil War was donated to the city in 1892 by the Starr King Monument Committee.

The inscription on the base of the statue reads: "In whom benevolence, strength and virtue were devoted with courage to truth, country and his fellow men."

PHOTO: COURTESY CALIFORNIA PALACE OF THE LEGION OF HONOR

61 This portrait bust of George Louis LeClerc is by the French sculptor, Houdon, and is in the Collis P. Huntington Memorial Collection in the California Palace of the Legion of Honor, San Francisco

Thomas Starr King, French   62

The Doughboy

The Doughboy was sponsored by the Native Sons and Daughters who commissioned sculptor Earl Cummings to do the figure atop the rock, upon which is a bronze plaque bearing the names of their members who lost their lives in World War I. It is in San Francisco's Golden Gate Park on the Main Drive opposite Sixteenth Avenue.

Apple Press

For many years this piece by Thomas Shields Clarke was thought to be a "wine press" because California is noted for its wines. M. H. de Young gave this sculpture to the city following the Midwinter International Exposition in 1893. It stands in Golden Gate Park immediately in front of the de Young Museum.

Fresno's 50th Anniversary Monument

This two-piece monument, which stands on a small triangle of land at the intersection of Divisadero, Broadway and El Dorado Streets, Fresno, was erected in 1935 to commemorate the fiftieth anniversary of the City. The main part of the monument is a huge piece of native Fresno granite; the smaller part, which is placed some 40 feet in front of the main monument, bears the plaque presented by Post No. 4 of the American Legion.

Doughboy   64

65   **Apple Press**

IN COMMEMORATION
50TH ANNIVERSARY
CITY OF FRESNO
1885 — 1935
FRESNO POST NO. 4 AMERICAN LEGION

PHOTO: COURTESY CHAMBER OF COMMERCE, FRESNO

50th Anniversary, Fresno   66

Thomas Star King, Cravath

1824 - 1864

Completed in April, 1956, this statue of Thomas Starr King, designed and executed by sculptor Ruth Cravath, stands at the entrance to the newly built Starr King Elemenary School on historic Potrero Hill in San Francisco.

In 1860, Thomas Starr King, at the age of 36, came to San Francisco as pastor of the First Unitarian Church. Upon the secession of the southern states, there was increasing likelihood that California would join the Confederacy. An ardent Unionist, King traveled through the entire state rousing popular enthusiasm for the Union. It was he who organized the Pacific Coast branches of the Sanitary Commission (forerunner of the Red Cross) for works of mercy in the Civil War. He accomplished his great work in only four years, dying March 4, 1864. Like Junipero Serra, he is a towering figure in the religious history of California.

Ruth Cravath, a native of Chicago, came to San Francisco upon completing her studies at the Chicago Art Institute. She has been a member of the faculty of the California School of Fine Arts, Mills College, and the Dominican Convent at San Rafael. From 1937 to 1943 she served as sculptor-member of the San Francisco Art Commission. Her work has been exhibited at major Pacific Coast shows, as well as at the New York World's Fair in 1939. She created three figures for the beautiful fountain of the Court of Pacifica at the Golden Gate International Exposition, 1939 and 1940.

Thomas Starr King, Cravath

68

DAVID   MOSES

This is a reproduction of the original by Michelangelo Buonarroti executed in 1501. The reproduction from the original was executed by Professor Armando Vene, Royal Superintendent of Fine Arts of Italy. It is of Carrara marble from the same quarry as the original. See page 70. At the entrance to Cathedral Corridor, Memorial Terrace, forming a part of Forest Lawn's permanent collection of art treasures is this full size reproduction of Moses, done some four hundred years ago by the master hand of Michaelangelo, the greatest of all sculptors. The original stands today in Rome, in the Church of St. Peter in Chains. Picture on page 71.

THE CHRISTUS

The original by Bertel Thorvaldsen stands in the Church of our Lady, Copenhagen, Denmark. The full size faithful reproduction is a portion of Forest Lawn Memorial Park's permanent collection of art treasures. Picture on page 72.

ST. GEORGE

This reproduction of the nine foot statue of St. George, Christian Martyr, is said to be one of Forest Lawn's finest acquisitions. This statue, acclaimed the world over as one of Donatelli's great masterpieces, is the most outstanding personification of a Christian hero ever to be carved in marble. Picture on page 73.

FINDING OF MOSES FOUNTAIN

This fountain by Brazza is just north of Forest Lawn's administration building in Glendale. This reproduction was chosen for Forest Lawn's permanent collection as a companion piece to Michelangelo's Moses, it being the intention to show the lowly beginning of the Hebrew leader and later to depict him at the height of his glory.

David   70

71   Moses

PHOTO: FOREST LAWN MEMORIAL PARK ASSN., GLENDALE

The Christus

72

73   St. George

The Finding of Moses   74

Abraham Lincoln
1809 - 1867

This imposing statue of Abraham Lincoln, who was the country's 16th President, is on Polk Street in San Francisco's Civic Center, in front of the City Hall. It is the work of sculptor Haig Patigan and was dedicated in 1927. What Mark Anthony said at Caesar's funeral about the good men do living after them applies especially to Lincoln. For today, no man is more lauded, praised, talked and written about than he.

How one takes it would depend on which side of the Mason-Dixon Line he is, or was. Every school child knows Lincoln's Gettysburg address and there are few among us who have not read his masterpiece to Mrs. Bixby upon the death of her son in battle. Always remembered will be his campaign speech in which he said: "A house divided against itself cannot stand; the government divided into free states and slave states cannot endure; they must all be free states or all be slave states. They must be one thing or the other."

The literary skill which he subsequently developed was variously attributed to his reading of the Bible, Shakespeare and Burns, his favorite reading.

Abraham Lincoln, Los Angeles

This imposing bust of Abraham Lincoln is by sculptor Julia Bracken Wendt. It stands in Lincoln Park, at the intersection of No. Main Street and Mission Road. It was a gift to the city of Los Angeles by the late Dr. Norman Ridge. The unveiling ceremonies took place July 4, 1926.

75

LINCOLN
ERECTED BY PVBLIC SVBSCRIPTION
VNDER THE AVSPICES OF THE LINCOLN
MONVMENT LEAGVE REPRESENTING
THE GRAND ARMY OF THE REPVBLIC
& THE LINCOLN GRAMMAR SCHOOL
ASSOCIATION OF SAN FRANCISCO

MCMXXVII

Lincoln   San Francisco   76

PHOTO: FRANK THOMAS, LOS ANGELES

77   **Abraham Lincoln,** Los Angeles

PHOTO: FRANK THOMAS, LOS ANGELES

MIGUEL HIDALGO This magnificent statue of Father Hidalgo, Mexico's martyred patriot, was presented to the city of Los Angeles by its Mexican citizens. It stands in the city's Lincoln park.

78

General Ulysses Simpson Grant
1822 - 1885

A committee of San Francisco citizens, headed by Congress-man O'Connor, subscribed the funds required to com-mission sculptor Schmid to do this imposing statue to the memory of General Grant, who was our 18th President. This statue is in San Francisco's Golden Gate Park, on the Museum Drive.

Grant was graduated from West Point in 1843 and was a lieutenant with Generals Taylor and Scott in the Mexican War. After service at Forts Vancouver and Humboldt in Oregon and California, he resigned his commission in 1854.

When hostilities broke out between the North and South, he re-entered the army as Colonel of the 21st Volun-teer Regiment. Not long after he was appointed Brigadier General.

Grant made newspaper headlines when, on May 11, 1864, he wrote Major General Halleck, then Chief-of-staff at Washington that: "I propose to fight it out on this line if it takes all summer."

Singleness of purpose and relentless vigor in execution of the purpose were the qualities necessary to the conduct of the vast enterprise of subduing the Confederacy. Grant possessed or acquired both to such a degree that he proved equal to the emergency.

General Grant   80

General Henry Wager Halleck
1815 - 1872

Major General G. W. Callum commissioned sculptor Conrad to do this statue of General Halleck, and then presented it to the City of San Francisco. It is located in the Golden Gate Park on the south side of the Main Drive.

Halleck was born in Westernville, New York, graduated from West Point in 1839, and was appointed second lieutenant in the Engineers Corps. In 1845 he was sent by the government to visit the various military establishments in Europe.

Upon his return to the United States, he delivered a course of lectures on the Science of War, published in 1846 under the title: "Elements of Military Art and Science", a later edition of which was used as a text book by the volunteer officers of the Civil War.

At the outbreak of the Mexican War he came to California and was a staff officer and Secretary of State under the Military Government. In 1849 he helped frame the State Constitution of California. In 1854 he resigned from the army and took up the practice of law in San Francisco, where he built the Montgomery block, San Francisco's first fireproof building which was recently made historical landmark No. 80 by the State Park Commission in cooperation with the Society of California Pioneers.

At the outbreak of the Civil War he returned to the Army as a Major General. In 1864 he was appointed Chief-of-Staff, a post he held until the close of the war.

General Halleck   82

Brigadier General
Henry Morris Naglee
1815 - 1886

This memorial to General Naglee, a one time resident of San Jose, is in the nature of a seat in St. James Park. It has in its back a bas relief of the General. The sculptor or designer is unknown, but that it was erected at private expense is vouched for by the secretary of San Jose's Historic Landmarks Commission.

Naglee was born in Philadelphia and graduated from West Point in 1835. He served in the war against Mexico and subsequently settled in San Francisco, where he was engaged in the banking business.

Upon the outbreak of hostilities between the States, he re-entered the service, was in the Army of the Potomac and rose to Brigadier of Volunteers. During part of '63 he was in command of the 7th Army Corps. He was mustered out of service in April, 1864.

After this, in company with his two daughters to whom he was devoted, he toured Europe, becoming interested in the science of making high grade wines. Returning west, he purchased 150 acres of land near San Jose, where for a time he was engaged in distilling high grade brandies. He died in San Francisco, March 5, 1886.

General Naglee 84

Jack London
1876 - 1916

This statue commemorating Jack London stands in Jack London Square in Oakland. The Oakland Tribune tells us: "The original cast was created by Finn Haaken Frolich. The cast turned up in the Blair Estate in Piedmont, and when the estate was subdivided, the deteriorated model was found, and given to Trafford Charlton, who kept it for about 16 years. It was given to the Port of Oakland by Mr. Charlton. The bust was then repaired and cast into bronze by Lee McCarty of Santa Rosa, the unveiling taking place on November 17, 1954."

Joaquin Miller

This equestrian statue of Joaquin Miller is a sculptored reproduction by Juanita Miller, given by her to the City of Oakland in memory of her celebrated father. It is located in Joaquin Miller Park, Oakland. Miss Keek at Berkeley made the moulds from the miniature, and the castings were done by Americo Tovani, Oakland.

Guardian of the Waters, San Diego

This statue by Donal Hord is in San Diego's Civic Center. One wonders why, with all San Diego's garrison of Army, Marine Corps and Navy, some of these lads couldn't be induced to "walk post" on their waters.

John Mulkey of the Union Tribune says that this is the largest "Diorite" statue in the world. But "diorite" was just another big word to us so we looked it up. Here's what we found: "Diorite is a granular, crystalline, igneous rock commonly of acid plagioclase and hornblende." NEXT QUESTION.

85

Jack London   86

87   Joaquin Miller

PHOTO: COURTESY UNION-TRIBUNE, SAN DIEGO

Guardian of the Waters, San Diego 88

San Pasqual "California's Forgotten Shrine"

Seventy-nine years after the battle, the State of California, in 1925, placed a bronze tablet at the site of General Kearny's battle at San Pasqual. The memorial is on Highway 17, about six miles southeast of Escondido.

Writing in "Westways", December, 1955, Ted Krec of Long Beach, California, gives a vivid account of this historic engagement. The story is too long to quote in full, but the following extracts and quotes provide the highlights of the battle. In 1846 the United States was at war with Mexico, and the then Colonel, later General, Stephen W. Kearny, was ordered to march from Leavenworth to California and take possession. Kit Carson joined the party en route, and was killed in action. Coming in sight of San Pasqual, the Americans spotted the Pico cavalry.

The engagements which followed were disastrous. "The mauled dragoons camped on the battlefield and added up the frightful toll. Eighteen men were killed in the fight. Nineteen were wounded—three fatally—and one man was missing.

"But what of the 21 heroes of San Pasqual—men who fought, numb with cold, with firearms wet and useless and sabres rusted in scabbards? Their bodies eventually were disinterred and removed to old San Diego. They were good soldiers. When the command was 'charge' they charged—to help make California a part of the United States."

89

San Pasqual Marker 90

Admiral George Dewey
1837-1917

This statue was erected by the citizens of San Francisco to commemorate the victory of the American Navy under Commodore George Dewey at Manila Bay, May 1, 1898. The ground was broken by President William McKinley and the statue later dedicated by President Theodore Roosevelt on May 14, 1901. The sculptor was Robert Ingersoll Aitken.

The statue is in the center of Union Square between Powell and Stockton, Post and Geary. The land was presented to the City in 1850 by John W. Geary, first Mayor of the city. The place was given its name because of the pro-union meetings held there during the Civil War period. After the fire in 1906, the square was dubbed "Little St. Francis" because of the temporary buildings erected there to house the St. Francis guests.

George Dewey was born in Montpelier, Vermont, December 26, 1837. He was graduated from the United States Naval Academy in 1858.

Dewey served all during the Civil War and took part in the attacks on Fort Fisher in December, 1864, and in January, 1865. He was made a Lieutenant Commander in 1865, Commander in 1872, Captain in 1884, and Commodore in 1896.

After his success at Manila Bay, where he made big newspaper headlines with "You may fire when ready, Gridley", he returned to the United States. By special provision, Dewey was not retired, but served in the Navy with the rank of Admiral until his death January 16, 1917.

Dewey Monument   92

The Spanish War Monument

Most historians give slighting reference to the Spanish-American War. But they all agree on one point. It dates the beginning of the United States as a factor in international affairs. There was no draft in 1898, and the National Guards from all states, as well as volunteers who enlisted in the regular Army, were given splendid farewells and hearty welcome receptions in San Francisco when they returned from the Philippines.

California won its spurs for abundant hospitality. The Spanish-American War Monument, just below Market Street in San Francisco, in the parkway that divides Dolores Street, is a Tilden sculpture, erected in honor of the California Volunteers in the Spanish-American War. It represents an equestrian Victory of heroic size, with a young soldier marching alongside her.

War Monument Fresno

The Gatling gun pictured on page 95 is one of the few still in existence in the country, and was presented to Fresno in commemoration of the Veterans of the Spanish-American War. It stands on the mall in front of the County Court House in the City of Fresno.

The Gatling gun was invented by Richard Jordan Gatling in 1862, but the Civil War was over before the War Department got around to adopting it. It was soon adopted by almost every civilized nation in the world.

It whizzed out 350 shots a minute, and during the few artillery battles of the Spanish-American War and Philippine Insurrection, was a great noise maker to frighten friend and foe alike.

93

ERECTED BY
THE CITIZENS OF SAN FRANCISCO
IN HONOR
OF THE
CALIFORNIA VOLUNTEERS
SPANISH-AMERICAN WAR
1898
"FIRST TO THE FRONT"

U. S. W. V. Monument, San Francisco 94

95

PHOTO: COURTESY CHAMBER OF COMMERCE, FRESNO

U. S. W. V. Monument, Fresno

JOHN McLAREN The "grand old man" who was super-intendent of San Francisco's Golden Gate Park for over 55 years has been memorialized in this life-size statue by Earl Cummings. It was a gift to the city by A. B. Spreckels in 1944.

Rideout Memorial Fountain

This beautiful and impressive fountain is in the center of the music concourse in San Francisco's Golden Gate Park. It represents a huge bear wrestling with a vicious snake. The sculptor was Earl Cummings, and the fountain was a gift to the city by Corinne Rideout.

William McKinley, San Francisco

This statue of William McKinley is located at the Baker Street entrance to San Francisco's panhandle. It was a gift to the city by the McKinley Monument Committee and the sculptor was Robert Ingersoll Aitkin.

This statue of our 25th President represents "Justice" and to his party adherents it eloquently befits the man. But it was during his first administration that the ghost of "Manifest Destiny" arose and walked the earth. We are at heart a nation of Sir Galahads hell bent on rescuing the Holy Grail at whatever cost.

McKinley tried to keep us out of war, but the Congress declared war anyway, and the fat was on the fire. The Spanish-American war was a great adventure.

The mild and amiable President was shot by a demented anarchist at the Buffalo Exposition, September 5, 1901. Eight days later the President died.

William McKinley, San Jose

This statue of William McKinley is located in San Jose's St. James Park and was erected by the people of Santa Clara County in 1902. The sculptor is unknown.

Rideout Memorial　　98

99 **William McKinley**, San Francisco

William McKinley, San Jose   100

Father William McKinnon

This statue of Father McKinnon, by sculptor J. McQuarrie, was a gift to the City by American Legion and Spanish-American War Veterans posts. It is on the Main Drive in San Francisco's Golden Gate Park. Father McKinnon, who was Chaplain of the 1st California Volunteers, was the first Catholic chaplain in Manila, and was a great friend of the Filipinos.

Chester Harvey Rowell
1867 - 1948

Dr. Rowell was Editor and Publisher of the Fresno Republican from 1898 to 1920, and editor of the San Francisco Chronicle from the latter date until 1939. He received his Ph.B. from the University of Michigan in 1888, and was subsequently a graduate student at the Universities of Halle, Berlin, Paris and Rome.

Hall McAllister
1826 - 1884

One of the foremost citizens and lawyers of his time was Hall McAllister. His statue, by Robert Ingersoll Aitken, was a gift to the City of San Francisco by the Bar Association. It stands on the north side of the City Hall, on McAllister Street, which is named for him. McAllister was the first Presiding Judge of the First Circuit Court ever established on the Pacific Coast, holding office from 1885 until 1862.

101

The statue inscription reads:

CHAPLAIN
WILLIAM D. McKINNON
FIRST CALIFORNIA
U.S. VOL. INF.
1898-99

Chaplain McKinnon

PHOTO: LAVAL CO., INC., FRESNO

103   Chester Rowell

Hall McAllister   104

Goethe - Schiller

Johann Wolfgang von Goethe is called by the Encyclopaedia Britannica "the greatest of German poets". Johann
Christoph Friedrich von Schiller was poet, dramatist and
philosopher. In the statue the two men are walking together, and this is as it should be, for they were friends
through a good portion of their adult lives.

"They first met when Goethe was writing 'Wilhelm
Meister' and Schiller served as an interested and con-
structive critic. Later the two collaborated on a magazine.
The relationship was highly literary and a 'certain barrier
of reserve' was always present." . . . From The San Francisco Chronicle.

This statue is located in San Francisco's Golden Gate
Park, on a footpath southeast of African Hall and the
Steinhart Aquarium. The sculptor was Reitschel

Portals of the Past

These columns are all
that now remain of A.
N. Towne's Nob Hill residence. Mr. Towne was one time
vice-president of the S. P. Railway. This memorial is on
the northeast side of Lloyd's Lake in San Francisco

105

Goethe & Schiller   106

Hearst Memorial Fountain

This memorial fountain to California's most loved benefactor is in San Francisco's Golden Gate Park, immediately in front of the Steinhart Aquarium. It was a gift to the city by Mrs. Hearst's admirers.

Phoebe Elizabeth Apperson was born in Missouri, December 3, 1842. She married George Hearst, June 15, 1862. Subsequently the couple returned to San Francisco, where their only son, William Randolph, was born April 29, 1863. Phoebe Apperson Hearst was a social leader in San Francisco, and when George Hearst was appointed to the U. S. Senate by Governor George Stoneman in 1886, her social duties were greatly broadened and she was then, as always, a gracious and charming hostess. Educational work, charitable work, parent-teacher organizations and many other activities to which a great-souled woman can give her heart and open her purse strings occupied much of her time and money.

The later years of her active life were intimately identified with the advancement of the University of California, to which Governor James H. Budd appointed her a regent in 1897. In this capacity she served the University for a period of 20 years. Her monetary gifts aggregated over a million dollars but these did not have the potency of her deep personal interest and her inspiring influence upon thousands of students.

Hearst Memorial Fountain

IN MEMORY OF
PHOEBE APPERSON HEARST
FROM HER FRIENDS.

Robert Louis Stevenson
1850 - 1894

In San Francisco's Portsmouth Square, Kearny Street between Clay and Washington, stands Bruce Porter's monument to Robert Louis Stevenson, who frequented the park and its environs for local color.

Stevenson was born in Edinburgh, November 13, 1850. He was ill most of his life, and came west for his health. Whatever may be the ultimate order of reputation among his various books, or whatever posterity may ultimately see fit to ordain as regards the popularity of any of them, it is difficult to believe that the time will ever come in which Stevenson will not be remembered as the most beloved of the writers of that age which he did so much to cheer and stimulate.

TO REMEMBER
ROBERT LOUIS STEVENSON

TO BE HONEST, TO BE KIND, TO EARN A LITTLE, TO SPEND A LITTLE LESS ... TO MAKE UPON THE WHOLE A FAMILY HAPPIER FOR HIS PRESENCE ... TO RENOUNCE WHEN THAT SHALL BE NECESSARY AND NOT BE EMBITTERED ... TO KEEP A FEW FRIENDS, BUT THESE WITHOUT CAPITULATION ... AND ABOVE ALL ON THE SAME GRIM CONDITION TO KEEP FRIENDS WITH HIMSELF. HERE IS A TASK FOR ALL THAT A MAN HAS OF FORTITUDE AND DELICACY.

THIS IS THE INSCRIPTION ON THE MONUMENT

TO REMEMBER
ROBERT·LOVIS·
·STEVENSON·

TO·BE·HONEST·TO·BE
KIND·-·TO·EARN·A·LIT
TLE·TO·SPEND·A·LIT
TLE·LESS·-·TO·MAKE
VPON·THE·WHOLE·A
FAMILY·HAPPIER·FOR
HIS·PRESENCE·-·TO·RE
NOVNCE·WHEN·THAT
SHALL·BE·NECESSARY
AND·NOT·BE·EMBIT
TERED·TO·KEEP·A·FEW
FRIENDS·BVT·THESE
WITHOVT·CAPITVLAT
ION·-·ABOVE·ALL·ON
THE·SAME·GRIM·CON
DITION·TO·KEEP·FRIE
NDS·WITH·HIMSELF
HERE·IS·A·TASK·FOR
ALL·THAT·A·MAN·HAS
OF·FORTITVDE·AND
·DELICACY·

Robert Louis Stevenson Monument 110

General John Joseph Pershing
1860 - 1948

This statue of General Pershing stands in San Francisco's Golden Gate Park, on the Academy of Science Drive just north of the African Building. The statue is the work of Haig Patigan, California's native son sculptor. The statue was unveiled November 11, 1922. It was a gift to the city of Dr. Morris Herzsten, a San Francisco physician.

Pershing was born in Laclede, Missouri, September 13, 1860. He was graduated from West Point in 1886 and was assigned to the 6th U. S. Cavalry. He saw service with his outfit in the wars with the Apaches in Arizona. During the Sioux uprising in 1891 he was in charge of the scouts in Dakota.

As a reward for his valuable services in the Philippine Islands, President Theodore Roosevelt, in 1906, promoted him from Captain to Brigadier General over the heads of 862 senior officers.

In World War I, General Pershing had a "few words" with the French on his insistence that the integrity of the American Army be preserved.

It was in recognition of his creating, almost from nothing, the vast structure of the National Army, that on September 1, 1919, he was made General of the Armies, a grade held only by one other American, George Washington. In 1921 he was appointed Chief-of-Staff and during his tenure of office he designed the new, permanent framework of the army.

General Pershing   112

Sausalito Memorial

Dedicated to their Comrades who lost their lives in World War I, returning Comrades erected this memorial in downtown Sausalito. The bronze plaque states as follows:

In Loving Memory of
THE SONS OF SAUSALITO
Who Gave Their Lives
In the World War

1914   1918

DANIEL FRANCIS MADDEN

JOHN NORWOOD McNEILL

JOAO DeCOSTA MOLLES

ALFRED HAROLD PANELLA

RAY HENRY VAN FLEET

Dedicated
By Their Comrades
Who Came Back'

IN LOVING MEMORY OF
THE SONS OF SAUSALITO
WHO GAVE THEIR LIVES
IN THE WORLD WAR
1914   1918
DANIEL FRANCIS MADDEN
JOHN NORWOOD McNEILL
JOÃO DaCOSTA MOLLES
ALFRED HAROLD FAMELLA
RAY HENRY VAN FLEET
DEDICATED
BY THEIR COMRADES
WHO CAME BACK

PHOTO: THE DARKROOM, SAUSALITO

Sausalito Memorial

Memorial to USS San Francisco

THIS MEMORIAL TO REAR ADMIRAL DANIEL JUDSON CALLAGHAN, U.S.N. AND HIS OFFICERS AND MEN WHO GAVE THEIR LIVES FOR OUR COUNTRY WHILE FIGHTING ON BOARD THE U.S.S. "SAN FRANCISCO" IN THE BATTLE OF GUADALCANAL ON THE NIGHT OF 12-13 NOVEMBER 1942, WAS FORMED FROM THE BRIDGE OF THEIR SHIP AND HERE MOUNTED OFF THE GREAT CIRCLE COURSE TO GUADALCANAL BY THE GRATEFUL PEOPLE OF SAN FRANCISCO ON 12 NOVEMBER 1950.

HONORABLE ELMER E. ROBINSON   MAYOR

HENRY V. CHESCOE
GEORGE M. CANTRELL   ARCHITECTS

Memorial to the Cruiser USS San Francisco

Lands End, San Francisco

116

General Douglas MacArthur

This imposing monument and life size statue of General MacArthur is in Los Angeles' MacArthur Park, better known to old timers as Westlake Park. F. W. Roewekamp, superintendent of Los Angeles' Park Development, states that the monument is the design of architect Harold Field Kellogg and the statue of "Doug" the creation of sculptor Roger Noble Burnham. A MacArthur Monument Committee raised funds for the purpose.

Douglas MacArthur was a phrase coiner from away back. His words, "I shall return," have made headlines in more newspapers than those of any other army officer, navy officer or politician. And he DID return to the Philippines and Japan a victor and much-decorated commanding general.

MacArthur, together with other allied dignitaries, received the surrender of the Japanese government aboard the U. S. battleship Missouri in Tokyo Bay. MacArthur's unarmed entry into Japan has been described by Winston Churchill as the "most daring and courageous" enterprise in the entire war.

Chief-of-Staff of the American Army longer than any other officer, more years of foreign service than any other, a long and brilliant career in the army, and at 75 an active executive in an international industrial enterprise, "An old soldier never dies — he just fades away."

STATESMAN

"COULD I HAVE BUT A LINE A CENTURY
HENCE, CREDITING A CONTRIBUTION TO
THE ADVANCE OF PEACE, I WOULD GLADLY
YIELD EVERY HONOR WHICH HAS BEEN
ACCORDED BY WAR."

SOLDIER

"BATTLES ARE NOT WON BY ARMS ALONE.
THERE MUST EXIST ABOVE ALL ELSE A
SPIRITUAL IMPULSE—A WILL TO VICTORY.
IN WAR THERE CAN BE NO SUBSTITUTE
FOR VICTORY."

General MacArthur

Florence Nightingale
1820 - 1910

This statuesque memorial to Florence Nightingale, founder of professional nursing, is at the front entrance to the Laguna Honda Home, at the corner of 7th Avenue and Dewey Boulevard in San Francisco.

The statue was designed and created by the late David Edstrom, and was dedicated on National Hospital Day, May 12, 1939, during the Golden Gate International Exposition under the auspices of the Northern California Federal Arts Project, Works Project Administration, City and County of San Francisco.

Florence Nightingale was born May 12, 1820, in Florence but spent most of her life in England. Working first in British Army Hospitals, she raised the standards of nursing as well as dietary and sanitary conditions. In her later years she remained a prisoner in her room, where she received favored visitors from time to time, never going out except for a drive in the park in the early morning. She was 87 when the Order of Merit was brought to her in 1907. Three years later she died in her house in South Street, August 13, 1910, and was buried at East Wellow, Hampshire, August 20.

Florence Nightingale, Los Angeles

This piece is by the late David Edstrom, the sculptor who executed the same piece in San Francisco. It was a Works Project Federal Art project, and was unveiled during the convention of the Association of Western Hospitals, April 12-15, 1937.

Florence Nightingale 120

121　　Florence Nightingale Los Angeles

Hunter and Hounds

This statue by the French sculptor A. Jacquermat was acquired by returned Veterans of World War I. The inscription on the base of the statue tells the story: "This shell-torn statue stood guard above a subterranean chamber in which Signal Corps, 3rd Division, American Army maintained Headquarters Communications during bombardment of Chateau Thierry, 1919. Second Battle of the Marne." Is in Beverly Hills, California.

122

Ludwig von Beethoven

Supervisor Emmet Hayden accepted this stately statue of
Beethoven for the city, which was a gift from the Beethoven
Maennerchor of New York. The statue is a replica of the
one given the city of New York by the same society, but
the name of the sculptor is unknown.

The statue was dedicated August 6, 1915, while the
park band played selections of the composer, who was
born December 17, 1770, in Bonn, Germany. Signs of
deafness had given Beethoven grave anxiety as early as
1798. For a long time, it is known, he had successfully
concealed it from all but his most intimate friends, while
he consulted physicians and quacks with eagerness; but
neither quackery nor the best medical skill of his time
availed him.

Guiseppe Fortunio Francesco Verdi

Over 20,000 persons attended the dedication of this 52-ton
statue of Verdi in 1914. Also present was San Francisco's
Tetrazzini, who sang a selection from Verdi's Aida. This
statue is the gift of the Italian colony, and funds were
raised by private subscription as well as from special
performances of Verdi operas at the old Tivoli. The statue
is the work of Orazio Grossoni, a native of Italy, where
the statue was executed.

His last work for the stage was Falstaff. In 1898 he
produced four beautiful sacred pieces, settings of the Ave
Maria, Laudi alla Virgine (words from Dante's Paradiso),
the Stabat Mater and the Te Deum; the first two for
voices alone, and the last two for voices and orchestra. He
died in Milan on January 27, 1901, at the age of 88.

123

Ludwig von Beethoven   124

125 Guiseppe Fortunio Francesco Verdi

VIRGIN AND CHILD This figure by an anonymous sculptor of the Picardy school was a gift to the California Palace of the Legion of Honor by M. Demotte. **126**

Major Charles Lee Tilden

This bust of Major Charles Lee Tilden, who, prior to his death, was the last surviving member of the first graduating class of the University of California, is in front of the Brazilian Room in Tilden Regional Park, Oakland, California.

The sculptors were Mr. and Mrs. Holger Jenson of New York. With Judge Donald Quayle heading the drive, a public subscription raised the funds and the statue was presented to the City of Oakland in 1950.

Major Tilden retired from active business life in 1946 but he retained presidency of the East Bay Regional Park District board of directors, a title he had held since its organization.

It was Major Tilden who, almost single handed, started the work that made its creation possible. To him has been given the credit for obtaining the consent of the board of directors of the East Bay Municipal Utility District to sell hill lands for park purposes. That was not an easy task, for the utility directors, at first, were reluctant to dispose of any of those lands.

It was Major Tilden who aroused public interest in the project, got the park measure on the ballot and finally spearheaded the drive that resulted in the district's creation. As a tribute to his effort, the largest park within the area was named by the park directors Tilden Park.

MAJ CHARLES LEE TILDEN
1857 — 1950
FIRST PRESIDENT EAST BAY REGIONAL PARK DISTRICT
DEDICATED BY HIS FRIENDS — JULY 20, 1950

Major Tilden   **128**

A. J. STEVENS

129

This statue by Albert Weiner of San Francisco is in Sacramento's Plaza Park. It was dedicated November 28, 1889. It was a gift from fellow workers of Mr. Stevens, who was with the Southern Pacific Railway.

WM. F. COLEMAN Memorial Fountain, by Ralph Stackpole, is in Sacramento's Plaza Park. It is a beautiful piece of work, and was a gift from Mr. Coleman's widow, Florence, in memory of her husband.

James Abram Garfield

1831 - 1881

This impressive statue of our 20th President is on the Main Drive, just above the conservatory of San Francisco's Golden Gate Park. A Garfield monument committee raised the funds for this work. Frank Happersberger, a native of Dutch Flat, California, was the sculptor. The monument was cast in Munich.

Garfield's tenure of office was short. He was inaugurated on March 4, 1881, and was shot July 2, 1881. He was shot while waiting for a train in a Washington railway station by Charles J. Guiteau. He died September 18th and was succeeded by Chester Alan Arthur.

PHOTO: COURTESY CALIFORNIA PALACE OF THE LEGION OF HONOR

131 This portrait bust of Louis XV is of bronze and is the work of the French sculptor Lemoyne. It is a part of the Collis P. Huntington Collection in the California Palace of the Legion of Honor, San Francisco.

Garfield Monument   132

The Shades - Raphael Weill

The "Shades," by Auguste Rodin, who also created "The Thinker," is in San Francisco's Lincoln Park, and was erected in memory of Raphael Weill, a pioneer merchant and citizen of San Francisco. The inscription is as follows:

MDCCCXXXVII
To
RAPHAEL WEILL
Officier de la Legion D'Honneur
Native of France
From His Manhood an American Citizen
Patriotic - Philanthropic - Art Loving
Sometime Member of the
Board of Education
This Memorial Is Erected by the People
of San Francisco
As a Token of Their Affection
MCMXX

THE SHADES
BY AUGUSTE RODIN, SCULPTOR

The Shades - Raphael Weill

134

The Pioneer Monument

This monument, located in San Francisco, at the south-eastern corner of Marshall Square, Hyde Street from Fulton to Grove, and extending to Larkin Street, is sometimes called the "Lick Monument" because it was donated to the City in 1894 by James Lick, founder of the Lick Observatory.

It is the work of Frank Happersberger and is really a group of five monuments, the central figure representing California and the others characterizing significant periods in the State's history.

Native Sons Monument

In the Memorial Grove, off the Main Drive of San Francisco's Golden Gate Park is this monument by Douglas Tilden. The monument was a gift to San Francisco by James Phelan, then Mayor, and stood at the intersection of Mason, Turk and Market Streets for over a half century.

Horse and buggy days passed and the statue in the middle of the street conflicted with motor traffic, so the Native Sons and Daughters had it moved to is present location in the park. The monument is a tall granite shaft surmounted by a bronze figure holding an open book inscribed, "September 9, 1850", the date California was admitted to the Union. Below stands a male figure holding the flag with a new star for California.

Pioneer Monument   136

137   Native Sons

THE DONAHUE MONUMENT   This statue stands at the intersection of Market, Bush and Battery streets in San Francisco. Executed in bronze by Douglas Tilden, it is dedicated to Peter Donahue, founder of the city's first iron works.

Ralston Monument

This Ralston Memorial is in San Francisco's Marina Park. It is the work of Haig Patigan and was a gift to the city by Major Edward Bowes.

In his recent book, "Comstock Commotion" Lucius Beebe has the following to say about the funeral of William Ralston, noted San Francisco financier. "Tom Fitch of the Virginia City Union pronounced the eulogy in the grand manner. 'Commerce commemorated his deeds with her whitening sails and her laden wharves. There are churches whose heaven-kissed spires chronicle his donations ... He was the supporter of art; science leaned on him while her vision swept infinity. The footsteps of progress have been sandled with his silver. He was the life-blood of enterprise; he was the vigor of all progress; he was the epitome and representative of all that was broadening and uplifting in the life of California.'"

The Man Who Built San Francisco

"WHATEVER HAS BEEN OR MAY HEREAFTER BE SAID OF HIS CAREER, ONE THING IS CERTAIN, HIS VIRTUES WERE EXERTED FOR THE DEVELOPMENT OF THE CITY AND STATE, AND ARE THE PRIDE OF HIS FELLOW CITIZENS."

WILLIAM SHARON

William Ralston   140

JAPANESE BUDDHA is located in the Japanese Tea Garden on the Main Drive of
141 San Francisco's Golden Gate Park. It is from the Island of Honshu, Japan. It was a gift to the city by Gump's of San Francisco.

SUN YAT-SEN is generally described as the "father" of the Chinese Republic. He was in England when the Revolution against the Manchus broke out, returned to China and was made Provisional President.

142

LATHAM MEMORIAL FOUNTAIN

This fountain was dedicated and presented to the city of Oakland in 1913 under the auspices of the Oakland S.P.C.A. It was donated by Milton and Edith Latham in memory of their parents. Monsieur Payre of Paris was sculptor.

143

THE BOY WITH THE LEAKING BOOT is on the mall in front of the County Courthouse, Fresno. The original was of pewter. This was cast in bronze for the Fresno Junior Chamber of Commerce.

144

Miguel de Cervantes
1547 - 1616

Cervantes, Spanish novelist, playwright and poet, was born in Alcala de Henares. He was the second son of Rodrigo de Cervantes. The exact date of his birth is unknown, but records show that he was baptized on October 9, 1547, in the church of Santa Maria la Mayor in Alcala.

This imposing statue is located in San Francisco's Golden Gate Park, on the North side of Museum Drive, just off the main drive. Two long-time Spanish residents, E. J. Molera and C. J. Cebrian, donated this fine example of the work of Sculptor Joseph Mora to the city in 1916.

Cervantes was variously a soldier, prisoner of war and literary genius. The conservative Encyclopedia Britannica states that: "The Novales Exemplares alone would give him foremost place among Spanish novelists. Don Quixote entitles him to rank with the writers of all times. Children turn its leaves, young people read it, grown men understand it, old folks praise it. It has outlived all changes of literary taste, and it is even more popular today than it was three centuries ago."

Don Quixote's Epitaph
(LAST VERSE)

NOR HAS HIS DEATH THE WORLD DECEIV'D
LESS THAN HIS WONDROUS LIFE SURPRIZ'D;
FOR IF HE LIKE A MADMAN LIV'D,
AT LEAST HE LIKE A WISE ONE DY'D.

BY MIGUEL DE CERVANTES

Miguel de Cervantes   146

Doré Vase This unique sculpture is by Paul Gustave Doré, illustrator of Dante's Inferno, Don Quixote and many other works. It is 10 feet high and weighs over 6000 pounds, is outside the de Young Museum in San Francisco's Golden Gate Park.

147

HARE AND CHILD This bronze piece, by Arthur Putnam, California's celebrated sculptor, is a part of the Spreckels collection in the California Palace of the Legion of Honor, San Francisco.

148

Memorial to
Volunteer Fire Department

This memorial monument to the Volunteer Fire Department of the 1860's is the work of the sculptor, Haig Patigan, and was erected with funds left by Lillie Hitchcock Coit. It stands in San Francisco's Washington Square, on Columbus Avenue near Union.

In the days when every important member of San Francisco's industrial and social life considered it an honor to be a member of the Volunteer Fire Department, Lillie Hitchcock was an Honorary Member of Knickerbocker Volunteer Fire Company No. 5.

Lillie Hitchcock Coit, nee Lillie Hitchcock, was a socialite of the day, the daughter of an army surgeon, but not a crackpot by any stretch of the imagination; she was unconventional, daring and supremely individual, but as Miriam Allen deFord sets forth in her analysis of her, "her oddities were those of a great lady who is not afraid to be herself."

IN THOSE EARLY DAYS, BEFORE THE FIRE DEPARTMENT WAS PUT ON A PAID BASIS IN 1866, MEMBERSHIP IN THE VARIOUS COMPANIES, ALL KEEN RIVALS, WAS AN HONOR EAGERLY SOUGHT AFTER BY THE WEALTHIEST AND MOST IMPORTANT MEN IN THE YOUNG CITY. SAM BRANNAN, FOR EXAMPLE, WAS DELIGHTED TO HAVE A COMPANY NAMED FOR HIM AND TO BUY ITS ENGINE. SAN FRANCISCO HAD ALREADY BEEN DEVASTATED BY FIRE SEVERAL TIMES; JUST BEFORE THE HITCHCOCKS ARRIVED, IN MAY, 1851, THE WORST OF THREE FIRES TO DATE HAD LAID WASTE ALL THE CENTRAL PORTION OF THE TOWN.

— MIRIAM ALLEN deFORD

PHOTO: MOULIN STUDIOS, SAN FRANCISCO

Memorial to
Volunteer Fire Department   150

Coit Memorial Tower

Coit Memorial Tower stands atop Telegraph Hill in beautiful landscaped Pioneer Park. It was designed by architect Arthur Brown, Jr. When Lillie Hitchcock Coit's will was read, one-third of her estate was left to the San Francisco Board of Supervisors, the money to be spent in some purpose of beautifying the City of San Francisco, which Mrs. Coit loved so well.

In her memorable book, "They Were San Franciscans", Miriam Allen deFord tells us that the tower "has been called 'the smokestack' in derision; and the tall cylinder, visible from every hill in the city, is not pleasing to conventional aesthetes. Five thousand years from now, should it remain amid the ruins of San Francisco, seventieth century archaeologists might be forgiven if they deduced that the barbarians of the Pre-Television Age were devotees of a phallic religion! But it provides the best—and almost the only—bird's eye view of all the city on its score of startling hills; and for that reason it may be granted that it 'adds to the beauty of said city' as its donor wished."

OLD ENGINE NO. 5 MANY YEARS AGO WAS SOLD TO CARSON CITY, NEVADA, LIKE AN OLD HORSE WITH A FEW WORKING YEARS STILL IN HIM. THERE AFTER A WHILE IT WAS DISCARDED AS OBSOLETE AND ANTIQUATED. SOME OF LILLIE HITCHCOCK COIT'S FRIENDS FOUND IT AND BOUGHT IT. IT WAS GIVEN TO THE DE YOUNG MUSEUM, WHERE IT STANDS AT THE END OF A LONG HALL, NEAR HER OTHER MEMORIALS. WHEN THE COIT TOWER WAS DEDICATED, ON OCTOBER 8, 1933, SOMEONE HAD A HAPPY THOUGHT. OLD NO. 5 WAS TRUNDLED OUT FROM THE MUSEUM IN GOLDEN GATE PARK, AND FOR THE LAST TIME IT WAS DRAGGED UP TELEGRAPH HILL. IT HAD ALWAYS BEEN THE COMPANY'S BOAST THAT NO. 5 COULD MAKE THAT HILL, EVEN IN THE DAYS OF BOTTOMLESS MUD, WHERE OTHER ENGINES BALKED AT THE LOWER SLOPES.

— MIRIAM ALLEN DEFORD

151

PHOTO: MOULIN STUDIOS, SAN FRANCISCO

Coit Tower   152

Fountain of the Turtles

The four children of Mr. and Mrs. William H. Crocker presented this statue to the City of San Francisco in memory of their parents. The Recreation and Park Department accepted the gift and the Art Commission approved its location in Huntington Park at California and Taylor Streets.

About this statue, a writer in the San Francisco Chronicle (no date on our clipping) has the following to say about this famous work:

"The famous group of sculpture called Fontana Delle Tartarughe, which the Crocker family just gave to the city and which now stands in flashing beauty in Huntington Park atop Nob Hill, is already causing comment from people who ought to know better. Such as the remark made by a man who stood and stared at it disapprovingly the other day: 'They should put swim trunks on those fellows; might corrupt our children playing in the park.' 'Those fellows' are youths in the fountain who are indeed naked—as naked as the day their sculptor, Taddea Landini, finished the original (which still stands in Rome), back in 1585."

153

Fountain of the Turtles   154

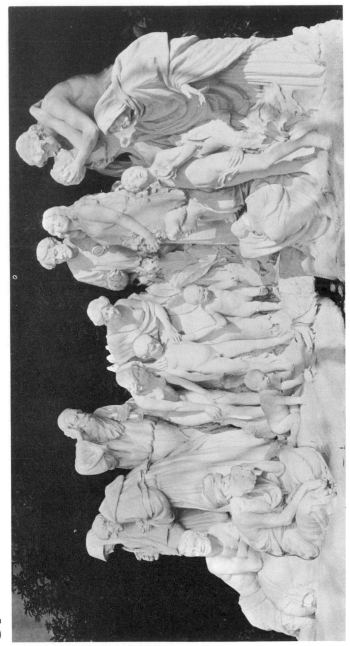

MYSTERY OF LIFE

This group is an original by Ernesto Gazzeri, sculptored expressly for Forest Lawn Memorial Park in Glendale, on whose grounds it stands, forming a part of the Association's permanent collection of Art Treasures, which is a personal project of Dr. Hubert Eaton, President of Forest Lawn Memorial Park Association. Dr. Eaton has assembled masterpieces from all parts of the world, making the collection in Forest Lawn the center of attraction for art-loving tourists in Southern California.

155

Dancing Sprites This group in bronze is the work of Henri Leon Gerber. The sculpture was a gift to the city of San Francisco by Mrs. James L. Flood, and is in Huntington Park, California and Taylor streets.

156

The Thinker by Aguste Rodin stands in the courtyard of the California Palace of the Legion of Honor, and was a gift to the city of San Francisco by Mr. and Mrs. Adolph Spreckels in 1916.

157

Roman Gladiator This statue is an "old-timer" and was a gift to the city of San Francisco by the directors of the Midwinter International Exposition, August, 1893, and now is in San Francisco's Golden Gate park, opposite the de Young Museum.

Shakespearean Gardens

Just south of the Academy of Science building in San Francisco's Golden Gate Park, is the beautifully landscaped garden dedicated to the memory of William Shakespeare. At the far end of this garden, landscaped with true John McLaren artistry, is a high brick wall with a bust of the Bard in the center. Flanking the bust, and inset into the walls, are four panels of bronze inscribed with Shakespearean references to flowers and plants.

The bust of William Shakespeare is the work of the celebrated English sculptors, George Bullock and Garrett Jenson. The bust was a gift to San Francisco's Public Library by the Mayor and citizens of Stratford-on-Avon, Shakespeare's birthplace.

It is a terrible indictment that vandals have so marked and otherwise defaced this magnificent bust that the Park Authorities have found it necessary to keep the bust behind heavy steel doors which are always closed and locked. The doors themselves are badly defaced with initials and other writings. There is no accounting for some irresponsible visitors who seem to delight in defacing public art treasures.

ON THE SIX BRONZE TABLETS FLANKING SHAKESPEARE'S BUST ARE SELECTED QUOTES FROM HIS WORKS. THE TWO FOLLOWING ARE CHOSEN FROM THOSE ON THE FIRST TABLET:

"AND IN HIS BLOOD THAT ON THE GROUND LAY SPILLED A PURPLE FLOWER SPRUNG UP, CHEQUER'D WITH WHITE"   VENUS AND ADONIS L. 1156

"AN EVIL SOUL PRODUCING HOLY WITNESS IS LIKE— A GOODLY APPLE, ROTTEN AT THE HEART."
                    THE MERCHANT OF VENICE I-3

Shakespearean Gardens

160

VENUS AND ADONIS This magnificent bronze sculpture was executed by an unknown

161 Frenchman in the late 17th or early 18th century. It is a part of the Collis P. Huntington Memorial Collection.

SELENE AND ENDYMION

This piece is the work of an unknown French sculptor of the late 17th or early 18th century. It is of bronze and is a part of the Collis P. Huntington Memorial Collection.

162

California Palace $^{of}_{the}$ Legion of Honor

163 The picture shows only the gate to the main building which was designed by architect Henri Guliiaume. This was a gift to the city of San Francisco by Alma Spreckels. It is in Lincoln Park overlooking the Pacific Ocean.

Palace of Fine Arts. This magnificent old building is in San Francisco's Marina Park. It was designed by architect Bernard R. Meyback for the Panama-Pacific International Exposition. Some San Franciscans want this stately old structure preserved and others desire it demolished.

164

JOAN OF ARC

165

This imposing bronze equestrienne statue of the "Maid of Orleans" is the work of Anna Hyatt Huntington. It was presented to the California Palace of the Legion of Honor by Archer M. Huntington in 1926.

El Cid Campeador
San Francisco

This equestrian statue of the Spanish hero is by Anna Hyatt Huntington, and was a gift to the California Palace of the Legion of Honor in San Francisco's Lincoln Park by Herbert Fleishhacker in 1937.

If the youngsters should ask you, "Who was El Cid?", you can tell them he was the favorite hero of Spain and the most prominent figure in her literature. The name, however, is so obscured by fable as scarcely to belong to history. The Jesuit Masdeu, denies that he existed, and this heresy has not wanted followers, even in Spain.

The truth of the matter has been expressed by Cervantes, through the mouth of the Canon in Don Quixote: "There is no doubt that there was such a man as the Cid, but much doubt whether he achieved what is attributed to him."

If you read Spanish, further information may be found in Castro's Las Mocedades del Cid. (1614)

El Cid Campeador San Diego

This bronze equestrian statue of El Cid stands in San Diego's Balboa Park, in the Plaza de Panama. This is a copy of the one in New York's Hispanic Museum. It was a gift to the City of San Diego by the sculptor, Anna Hyatt Huntington, in 1931.

Castillian literature begins with the poem, "Cantar de Mio Cid", the historical character named Rodrigo Diaz de Bivar. The Cid of romance is not the historical rebel, the consorter with infidels and the enemies of Spain. He is the type of knightly virtue, the mirror of patriotic duty, the flower of all Christian grace, the Roland, King Arthur and Bayard in one.

166

RUY DIAZ DE BIVAR

CALLED EL CID CAMPEADOR

SPANISH HERO CITATION
BORN 1040 DIED 1099

HENRY MEER CHAIR FISHER
THE A.P. DE LA MARE PARK

167   **El Cid,** San Francisco

El Cid, San Diego   **168**

LOTTA'S FOUNTAIN

This old-timer marks the intersection of Market, Third and Kearny streets in San Francisco. It was a gift to the city of San Francisco by Lotta Crabtree, a stage favorite of the 1870's. Originally a watering trough for horses, it was converted for humans by the "Path of Gold Festival" committee in 1916.

169

Ball Thrower

This statue on the Main Drive of San Francisco's Golden Gate Park is not a statue to ball players, but a monument to Douglas Tilden, the sculptor.

Tilden, a deaf mute from early childhood, was one of California's most gifted and beloved artists.

The Ball Thrower was presented to the city by James D. Phelan and placed in the park in 1892. The plate on the statue reads: "Presented by a close friend of the sculptor as a tribute to his energy, industry and ability."

Sun Dial

The Sun Dial, a gift to the City and County of San Francisco by the National Society of Colonial Dames, is a commemorative piece for three great navigators: Sir Francis Drake, Juan de Cabrillo and Fortuo Ximines. Earl Cummings, the noted San Francisco instructor of sculpture at the University of California and creator of some of San Francisco's most noteworthy pieces, did the Sun Dial in 1907. It is located in Golden Gate Park on the North side of Museum Drive, opposite the east corner of the M. H. de Young Museum.

San Francisco has long ranked with our first cities in public works of art. Civic bodies and public spirited citizens have given generously of time and money in the creation of statues and monuments commemorating noteworthy people and events. Despite this, the Sun Dial is a fine example of what immature minds can do toward defacing public works of art. Carving initials and obscene writings on public property is not funny and serves no purpose whatever.

171   **Ball Thrower**

Sun Dial   172

Hartnell College Panther

The huge black panther, standing on the lawn of the Hartnell College campus, Salinas, was executed by Raymond Puccinelli with Beniamino Bufano as artist-critic. This sculpture was carved from a 16-ton solid block of black granite. It was a gift to the college by the class of 1940, and dedicated in 1941 in ceremonies presided over by the late R. D. Case, superintendent of schools at that time.

"Peace" The Chronicle's gift to San Francisco

This 34-foot polished black granite and stainless steel statue, "Peace," will soon be erected in the landscaped forecourt of San Francisco's International Airport. The sculptor was Bufano, and the piece is a gift to the city of San Francisco by the San Francisco Chronicle.

The End of the Trail

When this book was originally conceived and first photos taken, this remarkable statue by the late James Earle Fraser was still in San Francisco. Now it has passed from the city and now stands in Mooney Grove Park in Visalia, California. The original is said to be in Boston, Massachusetts. It was the prize winning sculptor's dream to have the statue placed at the end of the Lincoln Highway, but the dream never materialized, and after being exhibited at the Pan-American International Exposition and the California Palace of the Legion of Honor, the statue was acquired by the City of Visalia.

173

Hartnell Panther

174

175

The Chronicle's Gift to the City — "Peace"

End of the Trail

176

Appendix

SCULPTORS AND ARCHITECTS

Sculptors

SCULPTORS AND ARCHITECTS (cont.)

Architects and Engineers

REFERENCES FOR FURTHER READING

THEY WERE SAN FRANCISCANS
by Miriam Allen deFord, 1941
(Revised Edition, 1947) Caxton Printers, Ltd., Caldwell, Idaho.

CALIFORNIA'S STATELY HALL OF FAME
by Rockwell D. Hunt, 1950
College of the Pacific, Stockton, California.

THE STREETS OF SAN FRANCISCO *by Samuel Dickson,* 1955
Stanford University Press, Stanford, California.

COMSTOCK COMMOTION *by Lucius Beebe,* 1954
Stanford University Press, Stanford, California.

FROM WILDERNESS TO EMPIRE
by Robert Glass Cleland, 1944
Borzoi Books, Alfred A. Knopf, Inc., New York, N. Y.

Names and Addresses of Professional Photographers Credited Herein

MOULIN STUDIOS	181 Second Street	San Francisco, Calif.
JAY RISLING	722 Montgomery St.	San Francisco, Calif.
LAVAL CO., INC.	314 Van Ness	Fresno, Calif.
FRASHERS, INC.	141 E. Second St.	Pomona, Calif.
HILLCREST STUDIO	Box 676	Angels Camp, Calif.
HURST STUDIO	112 South C Street	Madera, Calif.
BISHOP NEWSPHOTOS	4036 Arizona St.	San Diego, Calif.
TED KREC	2910 Pacific Ave.	Long Beach, Calif.
FRANK J. THOMAS	648 So. Broadway	Los Angeles, Calif.
DIV. OF BEACHES & PARKS	721 Capital Ave.	Sacramento, Calif.
GEORGE L. ABBOTT	Hartnell College	Salinas, Calif.
CONWAY STUDIO	900 N. Texas	Fairfield, Calif.
THE DARKROOM	3060 Bridgeway	Sausalito, Calif.

JACKET ART . . . . . ROBERT L. MIZE

END SHEET ART . SEWARD-WHEELER STUDIO

TYPOGRAPHY . . . . . JIM MELVIN

PAPER . . . ZELLERBACH PAPER CO., S. F.
WARREN'S SILKOTE OFFSET

LITHOGRAPHY . . . . MERRILL REED

BINDING . . . THE CARDOZA COMPANY

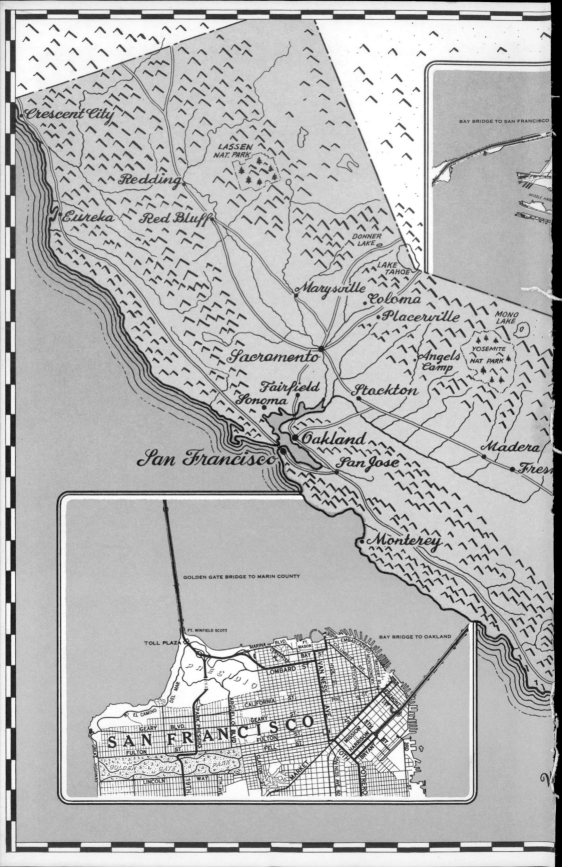